Design   David West · Children's Book Design
Illustrations   George Thompson
Picture Research   Cee Weston-Baker

The publishers wish to thank
Nigel Norris B.V.Sc. M.R.C.V.S.
for his assistance in the
preparation of this book.

Published in the United States in 1989 by
Gloucester Press, 387 Park Avenue South, New York, NY 10016

© Aladdin Books Ltd

Designed and produced by
Aladdin Books Ltd, 70 Old Compton Street, London W1

ISBN 0 531 17159 0

Library of Congress Catalog
Card Number: 89-50455

Printed in Belgium

Contents

FIRST PETS

Hamsters

Kate Petty

Gloucester Press
New York · London · Toronto · Sydney

Hamsters as pets

Hamsters make good pets. They are small, furry, quiet, and clean, and quite easy to tame. Most pet stores sell "golden" – or Syrian – hamsters. In the Syrian desert hamsters live in cool burrows and only come out at night. Pet hamsters sleep most of the day and wake up in the evening. Hamsters usually live less than two years.

Golden hamster in the Syrian desert

Some pet stores now sell dwarf hamsters, like this Chinese hamster. ▷

All kinds of hamsters

About 60 years ago a zoologist caught a family of "golden" hamsters in the Syrian desert. All pet hamsters are descended from that one small family, except for the Dwarf hamsters that come from China and Russia. Now, after many years of breeding, there are all sorts of colors to choose from. Syrian hamsters can be shorthaired, longhaired, or even satin-haired with a shiny coat.

Longhaired cream hamster being groomed with a toothbrush

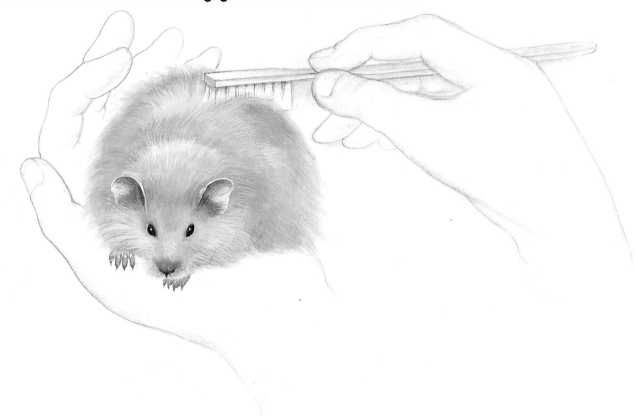

Syrian hamsters are no longer all golden. ▷

Secret hoarders

Hamsters are fascinating animals to watch. Sometimes they sit quite still, listening with their ears pricked up. Or they might be busy grooming their fur and whiskers with their paws. Most interesting of all is the way a hamster will stuff food into pouches in its cheeks. Then it carries the food to a secret store and sweeps its paws across its cheeks to empty the pouches.

Smoke pearl hamster
stuffing its pouches
with sunflower seeds

6

Black hamster grooming its whiskers ▷

Noises in the night

A hamster likes to exercise at night. Wild hamsters travel long distances along the tunnels of their burrows. A pet hamster might trundle around in a wheel at great speed. It can run surprisingly fast, too, once out of its cage. Hamsters are great acrobats. They use the bars of the cage like a climbing frame, climbing to the top and swinging along, paw over paw.

A blond hamster runs around in the safest type of exercise wheel.

A pet hamster exercising ▷

Food and drink

Hamsters need fresh food and water every evening when they wake up. They eat a mixture of grains and pellets and should have a few greens to keep them healthy. They enjoy gnawing on carrots and nuts with their sharp teeth. Sunflower seeds and fresh dandelion leaves are always a welcome treat. Beware though, as some wild plants are bad for them – and never give them onions.

There must always be fresh water for the hamster to drink.

A black hamster grasping its food with its paws ▷

The single pet

Syrian hamsters live alone in the wild and should be kept alone as pets. Two adult hamsters will almost certainly fight if kept together. A mother hamster will be fierce if she feels her babies are threatened. A frightened hamster bares its teeth – be warned, a nip can be painful. Dwarf hamsters are much more sociable. Unlike Syrian hamsters, they can be kept in pairs.

Hamsters fight with teeth and claws.

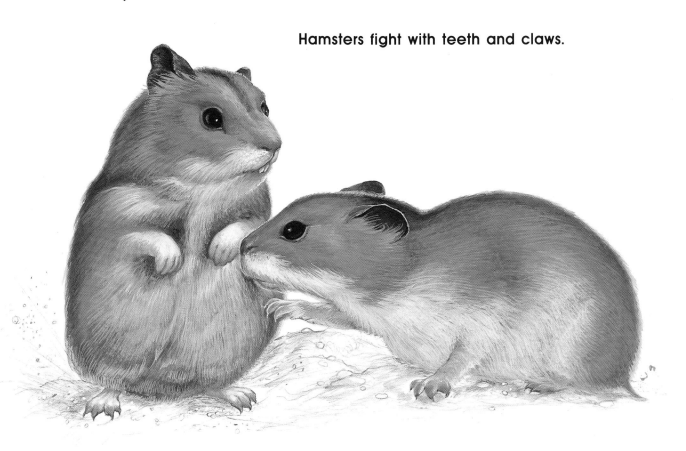

A cinnamon and white longhaired hamster on the alert for an intruder. ▷

Busybodies

Hamsters can be very friendly. They often show off for their owners by performing acrobatic tricks. They like to come out and be stroked, too. They are busy little creatures, always scurrying around with food or scrabbling about in their nests. They particularly like to shred white soft tissue and will enjoy playing with a cardboard tube.

Hamsters like to have plenty of things to play with.

Chinese dwarf hamster playing on a branch ▷

Newborn hamsters

A mother hamster has babies 16 days after mating.
It is best to leave her alone at first. Newborn
hamsters are tiny, blind and helpless. They look
rather like small beans. There are usually seven or
eight of them. The babies stay in the nest and drink
milk from their mother. She should be given milk at
this time in addition to her usual water.

Newborn hamsters are less than an inch long.

12-day-old golden hamster babies drinking milk from their mother ▷

Growing up

Baby hamsters nibble seeds at about 12 days old, even though their eyes might not open for another day or two. Once they can see, they start to explore outside the nest. At four weeks, young hamsters no longer need their mother's milk. By five weeks old they are ready for new homes. They are old enough now to have their own babies. A hamster is fully grown at 12 weeks.

The watchful mother picks up a baby that has strayed too far from the nest.

These babies are nearly ready for new homes. ▷

Handle with care

Hamsters become tame only if they are handled gently. They are easily frightened and need time to get used to people. Never grab a sleeping hamster from its nest – it may become upset and try to bite you. Once you have made friends, let a hamster climb on to your hand and lift it carefully out of the cage. Never drop a hamster – a fall can kill it.

Make a platform with your hands for the hamster to climb on to.

It may look like a cuddly toy – but its happiness depends on your good care. ▷

Know your hamsters

The original golden hamster from Syria is just as appealing as ever, but now there are many varieties of different hamsters to choose from. You might have to go to a breeder rather than a pet store for the more unusual ones. Chinese and Russian dwarf hamsters make good pets, particularly if you want to keep more than one.

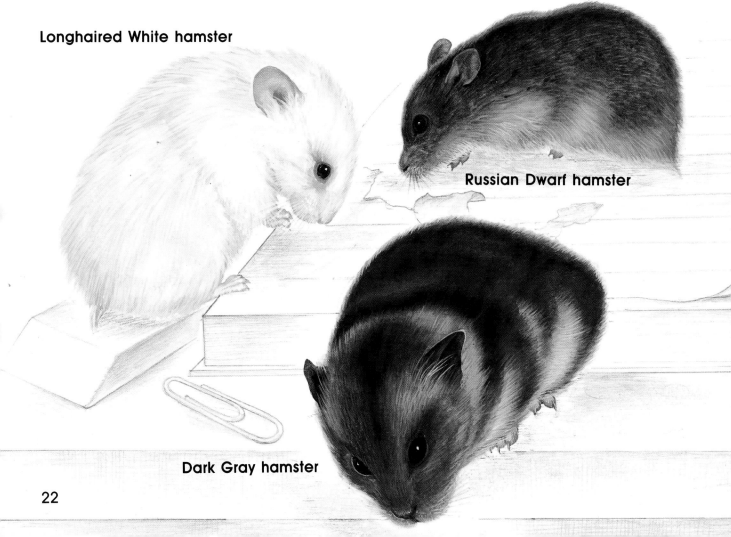

Longhaired White hamster

Russian Dwarf hamster

Dark Gray hamster

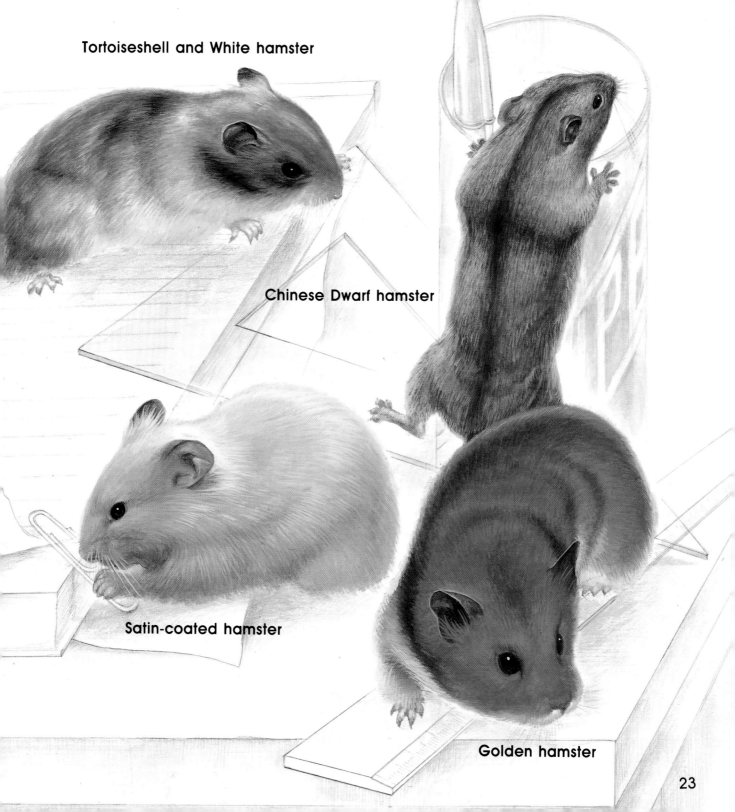

Tortoiseshell and White hamster

Chinese Dwarf hamster

Satin-coated hamster

Golden hamster

23

Index

All photographs supplied by
Bruce Coleman Ltd